I0777761

A Lecture on Popular Superstitions

by Bernard Whitman

with an introduction by "Black Books"

This work contains material that was originally published in 1820.

This publication is within the Public Domain.

*This edition is reprinted for entertainment purposes
and in accordance with all applicable Federal and International Laws.*

COVER CREDITS

Front Cover
Credulity, Superstition and Fanaticism. A Medley. (1798)
[Public Domain], via Wikimedia Commons

Back Cover
Hallowe'en Card (1909) by Raphael Tuck and Sons
[Public domain], via Wikimedia Commons

Black Books Logo
Candle Collection by VectorPocket, via FreePik.com
Vanitas [Painting] by Bartholomäus Bruyn the Elder, Public Domain
Marbled Pedestal with Old Books by Kues1, via FreePik.com

Fonts
Diehl Deco and *Attentica 4F* by Apostrophic Labs, via Da Font
www.DaFont.com

Research / Sources
Wikimedia Commons
www.Commons.Wikimedia.org

Many thanks to all the incredible photographers, artists,
researchers, and archivists who share their great work.

PLEASE NOTE :
As with all reprinted books of this age that are intended to perfectly reproduce the original edition,
considerable pains and effort had to be undertaken to correct fading and sometimes outright damage to
existing proofs of this title. At times, this task can be quite monumental, requiring an almost total
rebuilding of some pages from digital proofs of multiple copies. Despite this, imperfections still sometimes
exist in the final proof and may detract slightly from the visual appearance of the text.

DISCLAIMER :
Due to the age of this book, some methods or practices may have been deemed unsafe or
unacceptable in the interim years. In utilizing the information herein, you do so at your
own risk. We republish antiquarian books without judgment or revisionism, solely
for their historical and cultural importance, and for educational purposes.

Introduction

We at *Black Books* are pleased to bring you ***A Lecture on Popular Superstitions***, a wonderful old find from the early 19th century.

This book was written by Bernard Whitman, and first published in 1820, making it just shy of two hundred years old.

When explaining what he means by "popular superstitions" Whitman remarks "I mean all pretended signs of good and evil fortune."

This short old book covers aspects of well-known superstitions and their origins, and the author seems quite intent on debunking the entire notion of superstitions, putting belief in them down to a lack of sophistication and ignorance. The tone of Whitman's writing would lead one to believe that he is deeply offended by the very notion of a superstition.

The book, although written from the position of debunking, is a wonderful addition to the libraries of all those who study and research Mythology, Folklore and the Occult.

We hope you enjoy reading this dusty old book.

~ *Black Books*

ELOQVENTIA
VERAX

LECTURE.

Your attention is invited to some remarks on popular superstitions. I shall explain their nature ; investigate their origin ; describe their pernicious effects ; and propose measures for their banishment.

I. What is meant by popular superstitions ?

I mean all pretended signs of good and evil fortune ; all pretended influence of the moon and planets ; all pretended tricks for obtaining a knowledge of future events ; all pretended lucky and unlucky days ; all pretended supernatural dreams and visions ; all pretended witches and ghosts and apparitions ; and all pretended modern miracles. All these I class together. As they have been received for truths by the great mass of the people, I call them popular. And as they cannot be proved realities by rational and scriptural evidence, I pronounce them superstitions. Whether my definition be strictly philosophical or not, is of no consequence. You will all understand distinctly what I mean by popular superstitions.

II. What is the origin of popular superstitions ?

Ignorance of correct reasoning has given rise to many superstitions. Inductive reasoning teaches us to infer general conclusions from particular facts which have come under our observation. Let me illustrate this definition by an example. You know that water boils on the application of a certain degree of heat. You have seen this experiment tried many times without a single failure. You therefore conclude that water will always boil on the application of this degree of heat, although you have seen it applied to but a small portion of the water in creation. Thus you draw this general conclusion from the few particular facts which you have witnessed. But had you noticed several failures in the trial, your conclusion would have been doubtful. And if the experiment had failed ninetynine times out of a hundred, you would have adopted an opposite conclusion. You would have said that the application of the specified degree of heat would not boil water. In this way logical reasoning leads to the discovery of truth.

Now apply this principle of sound reasoning to the whole mass of pretended *signs*. Let me select one to show you the absurdity of believing in any. It is commonly reported that the breaking of a looking-glass betokens death to some member of the family. This sign probably originated in the following manner. A death happened to follow the breaking of a mirror. Some ignorant person immediately concluded that the breaking of the glass was a sure sign of death. The story soon spread among credulous people; and at length was handed down from generation to generation as an established truth. But you readily perceive the absurdity of forming this general conclusion from one or a few particular facts. For you know that death does not follow the supposed sign oftener than once in a hundred times; and therefore the breaking of the glass is almost a sure sign that no death will immediately take place in the family. But as mirrors are

always breaking, and people are always dying, it is not
strange the latter event should sometimes follow the former. It would be a miracle if it did not. But the events
have no connexion whatever with each other. The coincidence in any case is altogether accidental. And you
may say with as much reason that the breaking of a tea-
kettle is the sign of death, or any other event, as the
breaking of a mirror. But the truth is, there is no sign
in the case. It first originated in ignorance of correct
reasoning ; and has been perpetuated by the credulous.

Apply this principle of correct reasoning to every sign
in existence ; and you will find them to be superstitions.
You will find that they rest on no rational evidence ; and
consequently are entitled to no belief or confidence. If
they indicate anything, it is something directly opposite
to what is generally supposed. For they do not come to
pass more than once in a hundred times; and therefore
warrant a different conclusion. Not only so. If you believe in the present pretended signs, you may make a
million more equally good. A man quarrels after drink-
ing a glass of wine ; you may therefore say that taking a
glass of wine is the sign of a quarrel. A man draws a
prize in a lottery ; you may therefore say that the purchase
of a ticket is the sign of a fortune. A man dies after
supper ; you may say therefore that taking supper is the
sign of death. In this way you may multiply the number
of signs to infinity. And they will be just as good, and
prove true just as often, as any now in existence. But
our Creator has endowed us with understanding. He
has given us reason to regulate our belief by satisfactory
evidence. And if we do this, we cannot believe in *any*
of the pretended signs. We must conclude they have

all originated in ignorance of correct reasoning; and are kept in remembrance by those who will not use their intellectual powers as their Maker designed.

2. Ignorance of inductive philosophy has given rise to many superstitions. Inductive philosophy instructs us to trace effects to their true causes. Let me illustrate my meaning by an example. You know that lights have been frequently seen dancing over marshy grounds, near tan-yards, and burying-places, and along the sea shore. For a long time, credulous people considered them to be the spirits of the uneasy dead. This was a superstitious belief, because it rested on no rational evidence. Philosophy teaches us that these lights are occasioned by an inflammable gas, which arises from decayed animal and vegetable substances, and takes fire on coming in contact with atmospheric air. In this way inductive philosophy directs us to trace all effects to their true causes.

Now apply this philosophic principle to those superstitions which are founded on false causes. Let me select an example to show the absurdity of believing in any of the number. People have supposed that pork, killed in the increase of the moon, would swell in boiling; while that killed in her wane, would shrink. This opinion probably originated in the following manner. Some person killed, at different periods of the moon, two hogs which had been born and fattened together. That killed in her increase swelled in boiling; while the other, killed in her wane, shrunk. He saw no way of accounting for the facts, but on the supposition of lunar influence. This conclusion was accordingly adopted, and at length became an established truth. Now there was no philosophy in forming this opinion from a few such facts. More ex-

periments should have been tried.   And their results
would soon have convinced him that the cause of the
swelling and shrinking existed in the constitution of the
animals.   He would have discovered that pork of fine and
solid texture would commonly swell, whenever killed ;
while that of loose and coarse grain would as generally
shrink.   And his conclusion would have been, that the
moon had no more to do with his hogs than the Pope of
Rome.

Let this philosophic principle be applied to this whole
class of superstitions, and you will arrive at similar results.
It certainly boasts of many varieties.   There is the pretended influence of the moon on making soap, grafting
trees, cutting timber, and mental derangement.   Now
the moon probably exerts no more influence on any of
these things than the ghost of Bonaparte.   Then there is
the supposed special interposition of Providence.   A calamity befalls one religious denomination.   Opposing sects
pronounce it a special judgment of Heaven.   The same
thing afterwards happens to themselves ; and they, as
readily as inconsistently, interpret it to be a special token
of divine love.   For, say they, every child whom God
loveth he chasteneth.   A religious society engages in
some doubtful undertaking.   Their perseverance secures
success ; and this is represented as proof of the divine
approbation.   The cheating miser might as justly assign
the same reason for his prosperity.   There is likewise the
miraculous agency of the devil, as exhibited in fortune
telling, haunted houses, witches, and apparitions.   And
with all these things the devil has no more connexion
than the sea serpent.   To this numerous list you might
add thousands more.   You might call the flames of a

volcano proof positive of a material hell. You might attribute this mild winter to the choice of a southern president. But we have capacities for obtaining the truth. Let us not slight these precious gifts of our heavenly Father.

3. Ignorance of the causes of our dreams has given rise to many superstitions. Old divines inform us that some of our dreams proceed from ourselves ; others from the Deity ; and others again from the devil. They probably came to this conclusion in the following manner. They knew, from their own experience, that some dreams proceeded from themselves ; and this was assigned us the first cause. They learnt from revelation that God had made communications by dreams to some of his favored children ; and they inferred that he might do the same to others ; and this was regarded as the second cause. But as bad dreams could not proceed from a good being, they were under the necessity of attributing such to a different origin. And being firm believers in the heathen notion that God divides the government of the world with an omnipresent, malignant being, they concluded to give the devil his due ; and accordingly fathered upon him all those which could not be attributed either to themselves or their Maker. Their opinion has been extensively embraced, and has occasioned much unhappiness. But it does not rest on rational and scriptural evidence, and must therefore be regarded as an ancient superstition.

Have you satisfactory evidence that God is the author of any of your dreams ? I readily grant that he can suggest to your minds any trains of thought whatever ; for he is the omnipotent Ruler of all things material and spiritual. I admit that he has spoken to some of his dependent

children by dreams; for the scriptures give me this information. But you will recollect that such dreams were
direct revelations for the accomplishment of some divine
purpose. You will also remember that the volume of
revelation was long since closed; and that all which is
essential to the present and eternal happiness of mankind
is plainly revealed. There is therefore no necessity for
any further communications from heaven; and the gospel
does not authorise us to expect any. But if God has appeared to any one in a dream, it is a direct revelation;
and as no revelation is of private interpretation, he is bound
to publish it for general benefit. In such a case, he must
give us satisfactory evidence that this communication is
of divine origin. And this he cannot do, for on this subject, the bare word of no man can be received in evidence,
since those who have made such pretensions have eventually discovered their mistake. There is no criterion
by which to determine this question. And suppose some
remarkable dreams have occasionally occurred; suppose
they have sometimes had the appearance of being fulfilled;
what does all this prove? Nothing at all. For all this
can be satisfactorily explained on the doctrine of the calculation of chances, and the principles of mental philosophy, without resorting for an explanation to the miraculous
interposition of the Deity. And how great must be the
vanity and presumption of that person who professes to
believe that God has actually appeared to him, and really
addressed him, and made him the organ of divine communications!

Have you satisfactory evidence that the devil is the
author of any of your dreams? I am no where informed
that he possesses any such power of himself. I am no

where instructed that he was ever the author of a single dream to the children of men. I am no where told that God ever employs him in such business. So far as I understand the scriptures, I have every reason to believe that God regulates all the events of this world without his assistance or interference. If you say that he causes all those dreams that are not fulfilled ; then you admit that he has much more connexion with the human family than their own Father ; for not one in a million comes to pass. If you say that he is the author of all disagreeable dreams ; then how does it happen that these come alike to bad and good, and only when they are in some trouble of body, mind, or estate ? And how can you distinguish his dreams from those occasioned by other causes ? You have no means of making such a distinction. You may indeed guess that he is the author of a particular dream ; and your neighbor may guess he is not ; and on this question the guesses of one person are as valuable as those of another. And does it seem reasonable that a Father of infinite love would employ a malignant being to torment his frail children during the defenceless hours of sleep ? Is such a belief consistent with the instructions of our Saviour ? O no. You have no evidence that the devil is the author of any of our dreams. The idea is absurd. And it is unbecoming the followers of Jesus to harbor an opinion so superstitious in itself, so pernicious in its consequences, and so derogatory to the character of our heavenly Father.

We come then to the true doctrine, that our dreams originate from ourselves. Some are influenced by our bodily sensations. A person, with a bottle of hot water at his feet, dreams of ascending Mount Ætna ; and he finds the heat of the ground almost insupportable. Another kicks the bed clothes from his feet, and dreams of walking through snow banks, even in the summer season.— Some dreams are influenced by the state of our stomach and bowels. The hungry prisoner dreams of well furnished tables, and the pleasures of eating. The glutton dreams of a surfeit, and its attendant unpleasant sensations.—Some dreams are influenced by our dispositions. The person of amiable temper and cheerful spirits is frequently refreshed with delightful scenes and visions of bliss ; while the person of morose, gloomy, irritable, and melancholy habits, is generally harassed with those of a disagreeable and oppressive character.—Some dreams are influenced by the state of our health. Sickness is usually attended with those of an unpleasant nature ; while health secures those of an opposite description.—Some dreams are influenced by our waking thoughts. The mathematician solves difficult problems. The poet roves in elysian groves. The miser makes good bargains. The sensualist riots in the haunts of intemperance and debauchery. The criminal sees the dungeon or the gallows. The awakened sinner smells the flames of hell, or beholds the sceptre of pardon. The Christian anticipates heavenly joys. Finally—The occasion of some dreams seems as yet inexplicable. We are however under no necessity of attributing them to the influence either of good or evil spirits. For since we can account for so large a portion of them, it is rational to believe that the causes of the few unaccountables will be hereafter satisfactorily explained. We are safe therefore in believing that all our dreams are caused by some principle of our intellectual or animal nature.

But if this be the case, how can we account for the apparent fulfilment of some of our dreams? In three ways. In the first place, the cause of the dream is sometimes the cause of its fulfilment. A clergyman dreams of preaching a sermon on a particular subject. In a few weeks he delivers the discourse. His dream is therefore fulfilled. But his waking thoughts caused the dream, for he had meditated on this very subject; and they also caused its fulfilment, for he proceeded to write and deliver the result of his meditations. Dreams of this class are sometimes fulfilled at the moment. A student presented himself at Amherst college for examination. On the night previous to the appointed time, he arose in his sleep and proceeded to the President's study, who, being up, and perceiving the young man to be asleep, examined him in the various branches required for admission. He returned to his bed, and in the morning knew not that he had experienced any more than a natural dream. Such instances are not uncommon.—In the second place, a belief in the supernatural origin of dreams sometimes leads to their fulfilment. A person dreams of approaching sickness. His fears and his imagination hasten on the calamity. A general, on the eve of battle, dreamed of a defeat. His belief in dreams deprived him of courage, and sent a panic through his army. Of course, the enemy conquered. You also recollect the story of the German student. He dreamed that he was to die at a certain hour on the next day. His friends found him in the morning making his will and arranging his affairs. As the time drew near, he had every appearance of a person near his end. Every argument was used to shake his belief in the supernatural origin of his dream, but all to no effect. At last, the physician contrived to place the hands of the clock beyond the specified hour, and by this means, saved his life. There are instances on record where death has actually ensued in consequence of such a belief. It has been produced by the wonderful power the mind possesses over the body. And there can be no doubt that believers in dreams frequently take the most direct measures to hasten on their fulfilment.—Finally. The apparent fulfilment of dreams is accidental. The dream happens, and the event dreamed of soon follows; but the coincidence is altogether fortuitous, and is explained on the principle of the calculation of chances. A member of Congress informed me that he frequently dreamed of the death of some one of his children, while residing at Washington. The whole scene would appear before him, the sickness, the death, and the burial; and this too several times the same night, and on successive nights. His anxiety for his family caused his dreams. Now it would have been nothing strange if a member of his family had died. But in this particular instance it was not the case. In this way, however, we are always dreaming of our absent relatives; and it would be a miracle if a death did not sometimes occur at the time of the dream. So on all other subjects. But when one event follows the other, the coincidence is accidental, and not supernatural. There are occasionally some amusing cases of this kind. The best I recollect is the following. A person dreamed three times in one night that he must turn to the seventh verse of the fifth chapter of Ecclesiastes, and he would find important instruction. He arose with the morning light, and opened his Bible to the specified passage, and read these words.

"In the multitude of dreams—there are divers vanities." This is indeed important information for us all. And if we will take heed to it, and regard all our dreams as vanities, we shall be wise. Let us then pay no further regard to dreams, than to aim to have them refreshing and agreeable, by preserving a pure conscience, cheerful spirits, good health, and an empty stomach.

4. Ignorance of the influence of the imagination on the nervous system has given rise to many superstitions. I will give you a statement of some facts to establish and illustrate this position. My first example shall be given in the words of another. " Sometime previous to seventeen hundred and eightyfour, a gentleman in the city of Paris, by the name of Mesmer, pretended to have discovered a universal remedy for all diseases; and this remedy consisted in being *magnetized* under peculiar forms and circumstances. This *animal magnetism*, as he denominated it, he affirmed to be a fluid universally diffused, and filling all space, being the medium of a reciprocal influence between the celestial bodies, the earth, and living beings ;— it insinuated itself into the substance of the nerves, upon which, therefore, it had a direct operation ; it was capable of being communicated from one body to other bodies, both animated and inanimate, and that at a considerable distance, without the assistance of any intermediate substance ;—and it exhibited, in the human body some properties analogous to those of the loadstone, especially the two poles. M. Mesmer became so celebrated for this discovery, and he performed such extraordinary cures, attested by the most respectable authorities, that, in seventeen hundred and eightyfour, the French king appointed a committee, consisting of four physicians, and five mem-

bers of the Royal Academy of Sciences, to investigate this matter. Dr Franklin, then the American minister at Paris, was one of this committee. The committee, as soon as they had examined the whole apparatus employed in magnetizing, and taken cognizance of the mysterious manœuvres of Mesmer and Deslon, the latter a pupil and colleague of the former, proceeded to notice the symptoms of the patients while under the influence of magnetism. These were very various in different individuals. Some of them were calm and tranquil, and felt nothing ; others were affected with coughing and spitting, with pains, heats, and perspirations ; and some were agitated and tortured with convulsions. These convulsions were extraordinary in their number, severity, and duration. The commissioners saw them, in some instances, continue for three hours, when they were accompanied with expectoration of a viscid phlegm, which was ejected by violent efforts, and sometimes streaked with blood ; one young man often brought up blood copiously. They had involuntary motions of the limbs, of the whole body, and spasms of the throat ;—their eyes wandered in wild motions, they uttered piercing shrieks, wept, laughed, and hiccoughed. These symptoms were generally preceded or followed by languor, rambling, drowsiness, and even apparent insensibility. It was observed, however, that the least unexpected noise startled them, and increased their agitations and convulsions, and the patients appeared to be under the entire control of the magnetizer. They sympathized in his voice and every gesture. These were the effects of magnetism on those patients, as witnessed by the commissioners, and it was their office to investigate the true cause of these phenomena.—The commissioners observed that the great majority of those thus actuated were *females;* that they were not generally affected in this manner until they had been under the operation of magnetism one or two hours; and that when one became affected, the rest were soon seen in the same situation. In order to give the magnetizer the fairest opportunity to exhibit the power of his magnetism, and at the same time to obtain the most satisfactory evidence to the public, the commissioners all submitted to be operated upon themselves, and sat under the operation two hours and a half, but without any sensible effect upon them. The magnetizing instruments were then removed to Dr Franklin's house, away from public view, parade, and high expectation, and fourteen persons were magnetized, all invalids; nine of these experienced nothing; five appeared slightly affected, and the commissioners were surprised to learn that, in every instance, the poor and ignorant alone were affected. Subsequently to this, eight men and two women were magnetized, but without the least effect. At length a female servant submitted to the same operation; and she affirmed that she felt a heat in every part where the magnetized finger pointed at her; that she experienced a pain in her head, and during a continuance of the operation she became faint and swooned. When she had fully recovered, they ordered her eyes bandaged, and the operator was removed at a distance, when they made her believe she was still under the operation, and the effects were the same, although no one operated, either near her, or at a distance. She could tell the very place wherein she was magnetized; she felt the same heat, particularly in the back and loins, and the same pain in her eyes and ears. At the end of one quarter of an hour, a sign was made for her to be magnetized, but she felt nothing. On the following day, a man and a woman were magnetized in a similar manner, and the result was the same. It was found that to direct the imagination to those parts, where the sensations were to be felt, was all that was necessary to produce these wonderful effects. But *children* who had not arrived at sufficient maturity of age to be excited by these imposing forms, experienced nothing from the operation. The gentlemen of the magnetizing power, Mesmer and Deslon, asserted that they could magnetize a tree, and every person approaching the tree in a given time would be magnetized, and either fall in a swoon, or in convulsions, provided the magnetizer was permitted to stand at a distance and direct his look and his cane towards the tree. Accordingly an apricot tree was selected in Dr Franklin's garden at Vassy, for the experiment; and M. Deslon came and magnetized the tree while the patient was retained in the house. The patient was then brought out with a bandage over his eyes, and successively led to four trees, which were not magnetized, and was directed to embrace each tree two minutes, while M. Deslon at a distance, stood pointing his cane to the tree actually magnetized. At the first tree, which stood about twentyseven feet from the magnetized tree, the patient sweat profusely, coughed, expectorated, and said he felt a pain in his head. At the second tree, now thirty feet from the magnetized tree, he found himself giddy, attended with headache as before. At the third tree, his giddiness and headache were much increased, and he said he believed he was approaching the magnetized tree, although he was still twentyeight feet from it. At length when brought to the fourth tree, *not magnetized,* and at the distance of twentyfour feet from that which was, the young man fell down in a state of perfect insensibility ; his limbs became rigid, and he was carried to a grass plot, where M. Deslon went to his assistance and recovered him ; and yet, in no instance, had he approached within a less distance than twentyfour feet of the magnetized tree.—A similar experiment was soon afterward made on two poor females, at Dr Franklin's house.   These women were separated ; three of the commissioners remained with one of them in one chamber, and two of them with the other, in an adjoining chamber.   The first had a bandage over her eyes, and was then made to believe, that M. Deslon came in and commenced magnetizing her, although he never entered the room.   In three minutes the woman began to shiver ; she felt, in succession, a pain in her head, and in her arms, and a pricking in her hands ; she became stiff, struck her hands together, got up and stamped, etc., but nothing had been done to her.   The woman in the adjoining chamber was requested to take her seat by the door, which was shut, with her sight at liberty, and was then made to believe that M. Deslon would magnetize the door on the opposite side, while the commissioners would wait to witness the result.   She had scarcely been seated a minute before she began to shiver, her breathing soon became hurried ; she stretched out her arms behind her back, writhing them strongly, and bending her body forwards ; a general tremor of the whole body came on ; the chattering of her teeth was so loud as to be heard out of the room ; and she bit her hand so as to leave the marks of her teeth in it ; but M. Deslon was not near the door, nor in either chamber ; nor was either of the women touched, not even their pulse examined."

You notice that these effects were produced solely by the imagination. Those who believed in the efficacy of magnetism, and those only, were affected by the real or pretended experiments. And no influence could be exerted on any persons, after the commissioners had explained the cause of such effects. These facts exhibit very satisfactorily the power which the mind possesses over the body. A few more examples of a similar character may now be adduced. In a poor house in Haerlem, a girl fell into a convulsive disorder, which returned in regular paroxysms. On the next day another was taken; and so on, until all the boys and girls were affected in the same manner. No good was effected by any medical prescriptions. At length, Dr Boerhaave ordered several portable furnaces to be placed in the chamber. These were filled with burning coals. Over them were laid some crooked irons. The doctor then gravely commanded his attendants to burn the arm of the first child who should be seized in a fit, with the hot irons, even to the bone. This remedy proved efficacious. Not a case of the kind again occurred. Their fears were more powerful than their imagination.—In Chelmsford, a man had six children. One of them was afflicted with the St Vitus's dance. All the others caught the disorder by imitation and imagination. Nothing could relieve them from the malady. One day the father brought in a log and an axe, and solemnly declared he would take off the head of the first one who should exhibit any more gestures, except the one first taken. This declaration effectually cured the five. Their fears produced a deliverance from the nervous agitation.—In one of the Shetlands, a disorder prevailed among the women at church. When one was

taken, she would scream aloud. Others would immediately follow her example. The religious exercises were
frequently and seriously disturbed. At communion seasons, fifty or sixty would be carried out into the church
yard. There they would roar and struggle violently for
five or ten minutes. They would then become calm, and
know not what had happened. One day a rough church
officer threw a woman, who was often affected, into a
ditch of water. She was soon cured of her devil. And
the fear of a ducking prevented the recurrence of the disorder in any others. These facts illustrate the influence
of the imagination on the nervous system. More might
be added did my limits permit. But sufficient have been
given to enable you to explain many wonderful occurrences.

Now all those superstitions, which have arisen from a
belief in the miraculous interference of God, or the devil,
are satisfactorily explained on these principles. Take
first the whole class of supposed miraculous cures; such
as are said to have taken place at the tombs of catholic
saints; on the touch of kings; under the powerless prescriptions of quacks; and by the prayers of the pious.
Many such are on record, and their number is gradually
increasing. Some of the cases are too well authenticated
to be doubted. Many people have believed them to be
real miracles. But all such occurrences are clearly and
satisfactorily explained on the principles advanced re-
specting the imagination.—Take next the wonderful
convulsions, contortions, and agitations of body which
have occurred in times of religious excitement. Such
things have actually existed among several different denominations; among the Anabaptists, Quakers, French

Prophets, Methodists, and others. Many people supposed they were occasioned by the miraculous operation of the holy spirit. But they are now satisfactorily accounted for on the influence which the imagination possesses over the nervous system. Finally, take those occurrences which have been attributed to satanic influence; such as devilish visions, haunted houses, and witches. Some singular facts are recorded concerning these things. People have believed they were caused by the miraculous powers of the devil. But the subject is now better understood. There is no evidence to believe there ever was any such creature as a witch. All things relating to supposed witchcraft are accounted for on natural principles. The influence of the imagination explains the whole business.

[Those who would investigate this subject more thoroughly are advised to read a little book lately published at Andover, with this title : " Essay upon the influence of the imagination on the nervous system, contributing to a false hope in religion. By Rev. Grant Powars."]

5. Ignorance of mental philosophy has given rise to many superstitions. You know that many persons have believed in the real, visible appearance of visions, ghosts, spirits, angels, and apparitions. Now these things are clearly and satisfactorily explained on the established principles of mental philosophy. And from this source we learn that they *actually exist in the mind,* in the same manner as other ideas and images; *and no where else,* except in those instances recorded in scripture. They are caused by some mental operation or bodily disorder; and not by supernatural agency. My limits will not permit me to enter into a full explanation of the various

causes of their existence. I will therefore give a few examples, and offer such remarks as seem necessary to give a proper understanding of the subject. My first example is from the experience of one Nicolai, an intelligent bookseller of Berlin, who knew how to account for the appearance of his apparitions. Such extracts as are necessary to my purpose I will give in his own language.

"In the first two months of the year seventeen hundred and ninetyone, I was much affected in my mind by several incidents of a very disagreeable nature; and on the twentyfourth of February, a circumstance occurred which irritated me extremely. At ten o'clock in the forenoon, my wife and another person came to console me; I was in a violent perturbation of mind, owing to a series of incidents which had altogether wounded my moral feelings, and from which I saw no possibility of relief; when suddenly I observed at the distance of ten paces from me, a figure; the figure of a deceased person. I pointed at it, and asked my wife if she did not see it. She saw nothing; but being much alarmed, endeavored to compose me, and sent for the physician. The figure remained some seven or eight minutes, and at length I became a little more calm; and as I was extremely exhausted, I soon afterwards fell into a troubled kind of slumber, which lasted for half an hour. The vision was ascribed to the great agitation of mind in which I had been, and it was supposed I should have nothing more to apprehend from that cause; but the violent affection had put my nerves into some unnatural state; from this arose further consequences which require a more detailed description—.In the afternoon, a little after four o'clock, the figure which I had seen in the morning again appeared. I was alone

when this happened ; a circumstance, which, as may
easily be conceived, could not be very agreeable. I went
therefore to the apartment of my wife, to whom I related
it. But thither also the figure pursued me. Sometimes
it was present, sometimes it vanished, but it was always
the same standing figure. A little after six o'clock several stalkin r figures also appeared ; but they had no connexion with the standing figure.—The figure of the deceased person never appeared to me after the first dreadful
day ; but several other figures showed themselves afterwards very distinctly ; sometimes such as I knew, mostly
however, of persons I did not know, and amongst those
known to me, were the semblance of both living and deceased persons, but mostly the former ; and I made the
observation, that acquaintance with whom I daily conversed never appeared to me as phantasms ; it was always
such as were at a distance.—These figures appeared to
me at all times, and under the most different circumstances, equally distinct and clear. Whether I was alone or
in company, by broad daylight equally as in the night
time, in my own house as well as in my neighbors' ; yet
when I was at another person's house, they were less frequent, and when I walked the public street they very
seldom appeared. When I shut my eyes, sometimes the
figures disappeared, sometimes they remained even after
I closed them. If they vanished in the former case, on
opening my eyes again, nearly the same figures appeared
which I had seen before.—For the most part I saw human
figures of both sexes ; they commonly passed to and fro
as if they had no connexion with each other, like people
at a fair, where all is bustle ; sometimes they appeared to
have business with each other. Once or twice I saw

amongst them persons on horseback, and dogs and birds; these figures all appeared to me in their natural size, as distinctly as if they had existed in real life, with the several tints on the uncovered parts of the body, and with all the different kinds and colors of clothes. But I think, however, that the colors were somewhat *paler* than they were in nature.—On the whole, the longer I continued in this state, the more did the phantasms increase, and the apparitions became more frequent. About four weeks afterward, I began to hear them speak; sometimes the phantasms spoke with one another; but for the most part they addressed themselves to me; these speeches were in general short, and never contained anything disagreeable. Intelligent and respected friends often appeared to me, who endeavored to console me in my grief, which still left deep traces on my mind. This speaking I heard most frequently when I was alone; though I sometimes heard it in company, intermingled with the conversation of real persons; frequently in single phrases only, but sometimes even in connected discourse.—Though at this time I enjoyed rather a good state of health both in body and mind, and had become so very familiar with these phantasms, that at last they did not excite the least disagreeable emotion, but on the contrary afforded me frequent subjects for amusement and mirth; yet as the disorder sensibly increased, and the figures appeared to me for whole days together, and even during the night, if I happened to awake, I had recourse to several medicines. Had I not been able to distinguish phantasms from phenomena, I must have been insane. Had I been fanatic or superstitious, I should have been terrified at my own phantasms, and probably might have been seized with some alarming disorder. Had I been attached to the marvellous, I should have sought to magnify my own importance, by asserting that I had seen spirits; and who could have disputed the facts with me? The year seventeen hundred and ninetyone would perhaps have been the time to have given importance to these apparitions. In this case, however, the advantage of sound philosophy and deliberate observation may be seen. Both prevented me from becoming either a lunatic or an enthusiast; for with nerves so strongly excited, and blood so quick in circulation, either misfortune might have easily befallen me. But I considered the phantasms that hovered around me as what they really were, namely, the effects of disease; and made them subservient to my observations, because I consider observation and reflection as the basis of all rational philosophy."

Such is an abridged account of the apparitions of this philosopher. From these we obtain data for the explanation of others of a similar character. Let us then bring to this test some of those which were believed by the persons to whom they happened to be supernatural occurrences. My first example of this kind shall be taken from the life of Col. Gardner, in the words of his worthy biographer. "The Colonel had spent the evening in some gay company, and had an unhappy assignation with a married woman, whom he was to attend exactly at twelve. The company broke up about eleven, and not judging it convenient to anticipate the time appointed, he went into his chamber to kill the tedious hour, perhaps with some amusing book, or some other way. But it very accidentally happened that he took up a religious book, which his good mother or aunt had, without his knowledge slipped into his portmanteau. It was called, if I remember the title exactly, the Christian Soldier, or Heaven Taken by Storm; and it was written by Mr Thomas Watson. Guessing by the title of it, that he would find some phrases of his own profession spiritualized in a manner, which he thought might afford him some diversion, he resolved to dip into it; but he took no serious notice of anything it had in it, and yet, while this book was in his hand, an impression was made upon his mind, which drew after it a train of the most important and happy consequences. He thought he saw an unusual blaze of light fall upon the book while he was reading, which he at first imagined might happen by some accident in the candle; but lifting up his eyes, he apprehended, to his extreme amazement, that there was before him, as it were, suspended in the air, a visible representation of the Lord Jesus Christ upon the cross, surrounded on all sides with a glory; and was impressed, as if a voice, or something equivalent to a voice, had come to him to this effect. O sinner! did I suffer this for thee, and are these thy returns? Struck with so amazing a phenomenon as this, there remained hardly any life in him; so that he sunk down into his arm chair, in which he sat and continued, he knew not how long insensible."*

Now the Colonel would have us believe this vision to be a miraculous interposition of providence for his conversion. This he firmly believed, and his belief produced a happy reformation of character. But the whole affair admits of an easy explanation on the principles of mental philosophy. The Colonel had fallen from his horse a few days before, and probably injured his head. He was preparing for the commission of a heinous sin; and this too on the Christian sabbath. His conscience must have been exceedingly uneasy under his accumulated burden of iniquity. This book had probably awakened a train of thought, which brought forcibly to mind his early religious instruction, the anxiety of his friends for his reformation, some of the pulpit exhortations he had heard, and his base ingratitude and atrocious wickedness. All these circumstances operating together, produced this mental apparition—this vision which really existed in his own mind, and no where else ; and which was directed by an overruling providence to his present and eternal salvation.

As an offset to this, I will relate the vision of lord Herbert. This gentleman had written a book against Christianity. He was doubting about the propriety of publishing the work. I will proceed in his own words. "Being thus doubtful in my chamber one fair day in the summer, my casement being thrown open towards the south, I took my book in my hand, and, kneeling devoutly on my knees, devoutly said these words. O thou eternal God, author of the light which now shines upon me, and giver of all inward illuminations, I do beseech thee, of thy infinite goodness, to pardon a greater request than a sinner ought to make ; I am not satisfied enough whether I shall publish this book ; if it be for thy glory, I beseech thee give me some sign from heaven ; if not, I shall suppress it. I had no sooner spoken these words, but a loud, though gentle voice came from the heavens, for it was like nothing on earth, which did so comfort and cheer me, that I took my petition as granted, and that I had the sign demanded, whereupon also I resolved to print my book. This, how strange soever it may seem,

3*

I protest before the eternal God is true, neither am I any way superstitiously deceived herein, since I did not only clearly hear the voice, but in the serenest sky that ever I saw, being without all cloud, did to my thinking see the place from whence it came."

From this relation, you perceive that his lordship is guilty of a most glaring inconsistency. He writes a book to prove that there can be no such things as miracles; and then asks us to believe that a special miracle was wrought to encourage him to proceed in its publication. Still his sincerity is not to be doubted. His firm belief in the reality of the noise cannot be questioned. And his word is worth as much in evidence on this subject as that of Col. Gardner. But we know that God would not work one miracle for the conversion of a sinner, and another for the destruction of Christianity. The truth is, there was nothing miraculous in either case; and nothing but what admits of easy explanation on perfectly rational principles. There can be no doubt but the noise existed in the mind of his lordship, and no where else. And it was probably caused by his anxiety on the subject, his conscious integrity, his confidence in the truth of his cause, and other concurring circumstances. Both visions are satisfactorily explained on the principles of mental philosophy; and both relaters are permitted to retain their reputation for honesty and integrity.

On the same principles, I think the visions and apparitions of Swedenborg admit of a perfectly satisfactory explanation. His account of their first appearance confirms this opinion. You shall have it in his own words. " I dined very late at my lodgings at London, and ate with great appetite, till, at the close of my repast, I perceived a kind of mist about my eyes, and the floor of my chamber was covered with hideous reptiles. They soon disappeared, the darkness was dissipated, and I saw clearly, in the midst of a brilliant light, a man seated in the corner of my chamber, who said to me in a terrible voice, *eat not so much.* At those words my sight became obscured; afterwards it became clear by degrees, and I found myself alone. The night following, the same man, radiant with light, appeared to me and said,—I am God the Lord, creator and redeemer; I have chosen you to unfold to men the internal and spiritual sense of the sacred writings, and will dictate to you what you ought to write. At that time I was not terrified; and the light, although very brilliant, made no unpleasant impression upon my eyes. The Lord was clothed in purple, and the vision lasted a quarter of an hour. The same night the eyes of my internal man were opened, and fitted to see things in heaven, in the world of spirits, and in hell, in which places I found many persons of my acquaintance, some of them long since dead, and others lately deceased." In another place he observes,—" I have conversed with apostles, departed popes, emperors, and kings; with the late reformers of the church, Luther, Calvin, and Melancthon, and with others from different countries."

The apparitions of Swedenborg were much more numerous, and of much longer continuance, than those of Nicolai, but of a similar character. They were probably caused by his former studies, and habits, and pursuits. They bear internal marks of earthly origin, although he firmly believed they were from heaven. When examined by the light of the gospel and principles of mental philosophy, they appear to me to be nothing more than the visions and fancies of a disordered imagination.

My limits will not permit me to adduce any more examples. What I have said will be sufficient to enable you to offer a satisfactory explanation of all trances, visions, spectres, ghosts, angels, and apparitions. These things exist only in the minds of those who pretend to have experienced or seen them. They are not occasioned by supernatural agency, but by some mental or bodily cause. Those who relate them are honest and sincere, and firmly believe in their reality and divine origin. Such a belief has existed through ignorance of mental philosophy.

[Those who would examine this subject more thoroughly will find it fully investigated in a work lately published at Edinburgh, with the following title: " Sketches of the philosophy of apparitions; or, an attempt to trace such illusions to their physical causes. By Samuel Hibbert.]

6. Ignorance of true religion has given rise to most of the prevailing superstitions. Christ Jesus teaches us that our heavenly Father regulates the minutest events of this world; and that He alone is the supreme Ruler of the universe. Our experience and observation must convince us that this infinite work is accomplished by regular laws; and not by the intervention of miracles, or the instrumentality of evil spirits. Now these fundamental truths are directly opposed to the whole mass of popular superstitions.

Perhaps you believe in signs. If so, let me select an example to show the impiety of your belief. You say, for instance, that the howling of a dog under a window betokens death to some member of the family. How does the animal obtain this foreknowledge, or who sends him on this solemn errand? If you say his appearance at the house is accidental, then you would have us trust to chance for information on the most important subject. This is the height of folly. If you say his knowledge of the approaching event is intuitive, then you would have us admit that the irrational brute knows more than his intelligent master. This is the height of absurdity. If you say he is sent by the devil, then you would have us allow that the enemy of mankind is more attentive to their welfare than their heavenly Father; for it certainly indicates the greatest kindness to notify us of our approaching dissolution. This is the height of impiety. If you say he is sent by God, then how do you prove the truth of your assertion? Does revelation give you this information? No, nothing of the kind is taught in the Bible. Do the events follow the supposed sign with such undeviating regularity as to warrant a general conclusion? By no means. The sign is not followed by death once in a hundred times. And surely you would not accuse the omniscient and merciful Jehovah either of ignorance of future events, or of trifling with the feelings of his dependent children. Your assertion therefore is not supported by a particle of evidence; and these are the only sources from which proof can be obtained. Consequently, your belief in signs is superstitious, because it is retained contrary to rational evidence. It is also unscriptural, because it contradicts the instructions of the gospel. And it is pernicious, because it turns your attention from God to fate and chance and devils. If then you believe that the great mass of pretended signs is designed to give us information of approaching events, I wish you to answer one question for your own improvement. From what source does this foreknowledge originate? What being causes the signs?

Perhaps you believe in lucky and unlucky days. If so, let me select an example to show the impiety of your belief. You say, for instance, that Friday is an unlucky day. And why so? Does God permit the devil to rule the world on this day? This you cannot believe. For reason teaches you that a being of unchangeable goodness could give no such permission. And the Bible informs you that God never parts with the reins of his government. Does he employ wicked spirits to torment his children and frustrate their designs on this day? This you cannot believe. For reason teaches you that an infinite Father could not be guilty of such cruelty. And the Bible informs you that he loves all the children of his creation, and that his tender mercies are over all the works of his hands. Does God himself make this day more unpropitious to human affairs than others? This you cannot believe. For facts must convince you that no more disasters occur on this day than on any other. And Paul instructs you that all days are alike; and that God rules the universe every day with infinite wisdom and benevolence. What then makes this an unlucky day? You can assign no good reason. Your belief, therefore, that one day is better than another, or more unpropitious than another, is both unscriptural and irrational. Whence then came such an opinion? From heathenism. The heathen were much influenced by this superstition; and when converted to Christianity, they incorporated this with other absurdities into their religious belief. Because our Saviour was crucified on Friday, they placed this at the head of their unlucky days. Why they did so, I cannot conceive. For the death of Christ was absolutely necessary to establish the truth of his religion. And the day which contributed most effectually to its establishment was the most lucky day this world ever experienced ; as all must admit who will be at the trouble to compare the present state of heathen and christian nations. And for this reason, Friday should be regarded as the most propitious day. But the heathen converts did not consider this circumstance. They also pronounced Sunday, the day of his resurrection, to be the most fortunate. Later Christians have sometimes thought differently. Even the distinguished Hale has somewhere remarked that he never knew any undertaking prosper which was commenced on the sabbath. And the early laws of Connecticut prohibited any vessel from either leaving a port, or entering a port, or passing by a village on Sunday. But such prohibitions are now contrary to the wishes of seamen. You frequently meet with dissipated, unbelieving sailors, who could not be induced to put to sea on Friday on any consideration ; but who would rather labor seven successive nights than not sail on the sabbath. It is rather singular that infidels should be so afraid of the day of our Saviour's crucifixion, and so fond of that of his resurrection. Such inconsistency however is not uncommon. Those who make the greatest pretensions to liberality are sometimes the most bigoted. Those who rail most at the credulity of others are frequently the most superstitious. Those who lay the greatest claims to bravery are commonly the most arrant cowards. Voltaire could ridicule religion in fair weather ; but the moment a thunder cloud appeared, he was thrown into the greatest consternation, and must have a priest to pray during its continuance for his preservation. While in health, he could sneer at the most sacred things; but the instant death approached, he was overwhelmed with agony, recanted his infidelity, and died in the bosom of the mother church.—If then we would avoid the influence of this heathen superstition, we must regard actions rather than days. If our business is proper, we have nothing to fear from the day on which it was commenced. And if we feel that God is our Father, we shall not be prevented, by any belief in lucky and unlucky days, from doing our duty on every day, and enjoying peace and happiness on all days.

Perhaps you believe in witchcraft. If so, let me show the superstition of your belief. Your belief implies two things. First, that the devil possesses miraculous powers; and second, that he can communicate these powers to human beings. Now where do you learn that he can work miracles? Is he self-existent? This is absurd. If he is not, then he must depend on the Creator for his being, his preservation, and all his faculties. And where do you learn that God has endowed him with miraculous powers? In the book of revelation? No. Nothing of the kind is there recorded. Can you support the position by an appeal to facts? You can relate witch stories. And what do these prove? That those who believe them are exceedingly superstitious. They were caused by the influence of the imagination in connexion with a belief in their possibility and reality. And these are no evidence at all in the case. So that the opinion is not supported either by reason, or facts, or scripture. But this is not all. Once admit that the devil can work miracles, and you destroy all foundation for belief in revelation. For how can you tell whether any particular miracle be from

God or the devil? And if the devil can convert himself into an angel of light, how can you prove that he is not the author of Christianity? You see that such an admission would strike a death blow to all belief in divine communications. Well then, if his satanic excellence does not possess miraculous powers, he cannot impart them to others. And consequently there can never exist such a thing as a witch; that is, a woman endowed by the devil with a knowledge of distant and future events, and the power of working miracles. A belief in witchcraft is accordingly a superstition. And as the pure light of the gospel prevails, it vanishes from the world. The pure light of the gospel I say. For mere intellectual cultivation is not sufficient. Who were ever better educated than the ancient Grecians and Romans? And who were ever more influenced by a belief in signs, and omens, and spectres, and witches? Read the younger Pliny's account of the haunted house and supernatural dreams. False views of the gospel will not effect the object. For who ever had more to do with the devil than many protestant Christians? Read, especially, the writings of Luther. For him to have an encounter with the old serpent in a bodily form was the most common thing in the world. The pure instructions of Jesus will destroy satan and all his works. Be ye learned or ignorant, if ye believe that your heavenly Father regulates all the events of this world, you will have no fears of witches or devils.

But perhaps you ask how the subject of witchcraft came to be introduced into the Bible? If there cannot be any such beings as witches, why did Moses forbid a witch to live? The Jews knew nothing of divination until their connexion with heathen nations. Among them they found a class of necromancers and soothsayers, who pretended to foretell future events and raise the dead. The profession was taken up by some of the favored people. And by means of one deceptive art and another, and especially by means of ventriloquism, they succeeded in deceiving many, and turning them from the living God to such lying vanities. Of this class was the famous witch of Endor. Saul had ordered all such characters to be destroyed. Finding himself forsaken by Jehovah, he resolved to consult this fortune-teller. He attempted to disguise himself; and accordingly she pretended not to know him. But this was mere pretence. For he was a head taller than any other person; and he promised her security in the royal manner. In order to convince him of her miraculous powers, she pretended that some spirits had informed her who he was. This device completely succeeded with the frightened, depressed king. She then made him believe her conversation was carried on with the prophet, which was easily effected by means of ventriloquism. Her prediction was founded on such evidence as she possessed, and proved to be well founded. A more full explanation of the whole affair may be found in some of the late publications. And now what were the crimes for which this class of imposters were condemned to death. They were three. First, they denied the overruling providence of Jehovah. Second, they introduced other deities. And third, they seduced the people from the service of the one only living and true God. The very law of Moses goes on the supposition that no being but Jehovah could either foretell future events or work miracles. And if I pretend that the devil possesses miraculous powers, and can communicate these powers to human beings, I am guilty of precisely the same crimes for which the ancient witches were condemned to death.

Perhaps you believe in modern miracles. If so, let me show the superstition of your belief. In the first place, Jesus gave no intimation that miracles should continue after the establishment of Christianity. He promised to be with his apostles even unto the end of that age. He declared that all who believed their instructions should also have power to cast out devils, heal diseases, speak with new tongues and withstand any deadly thing. But his promise did not extend beyond the immediate converts of the apostles. And we have no satisfactory evidence that miracles were wrought by any but these; while we have abundant testimony that our Saviour's promise was literally fulfilled.—In the second place, there was no necessity for miracles after the establishment of Christianity. They were first wrought by Almighty God to confirm the mission of his well beloved Son; to prove to the world that he was sent by the universal Father to be the Saviour of the human family. They were continued to enable the apostles and their converts to propagate the new religion among all nations. When these two objects were accomplished, there was no further necessity for miraculous interposition. For a history of the divine revelation was committed to writing, and translated into the prevailing languages of the civilized world. And if any one would not be convinced of its divine origin by the mass of evidence with which it was accompanied, neither would he believe, though one should rise from the dead.— In the third place, the purposes for which modern miracles are said to have been wrought are not worthy the interposition of the Deity. Opposing sects of Christians have pretended that miracles have been wrought to establish the truth of their peculiar views of the gospel. This is impossible; for no sect can claim the whole truth; and the points of difference could not be true in two differing sects. Besides, a being of infinite wisdom would not give a revelation so imperfect or obscure as to endanger the happiness of any honest inquirer. Neither would he give one so powerless in evidence or efficacy as to require new miracles for the conversion of unbelievers. To confirm and establish Christianity was indeed an object worthy his miraculous interposition; as all must admit who will compare our elevated station with the mental and moral degradation of all heathen nations.—In the fourth place, pretended modern miracles admit of easy explanation on natural principles. Diseases have been suddenly healed; but imagination effected the cure. Religious excitements have existed among all denominations; but they have been produced by human exertions and concurring circumstances. Visions, ghosts, and apparitions have been seen; but they existed only in the minds of the observers; and were caused by some mental or bodily operation. Nothing of this kind can be said of the miracles of Jesus. His cannot be accounted for on any natural principles; but must have been caused by divine miraculous agency.—Finally, modern miracles are not supported by satisfactory evidence. They have been mostly wrought in secret. No witnesses can be produced but the most interested. This was not the case with those of our Saviour. They were performed openly; and in the presence of friends and enemies. They could not be deceptions; for the resurrection of a dead person could be tested by the evidence of the senses. The remark of the late lamented Judge Howe may be appropriately introduced in this connexion. He had studied the evidences of Christianity most thoroughly and impartially; and a firm belief in its divine origin was the result. He observed that no jury could be found, who would give a verdict against the truth of Christianity, if the evidences on both sides could be fairly presented before them, and they were governed in forming their opinion by the common rules of belief. The truth of this observation is confirmed by the fact that candid inquirers after truth have uniformly risen from an examination of the evidences of Christianity, believers in its divine origin. Now nothing of the kind can be said of modern miracles. No jury could be obtained of disinterested persons who would give a verdict in their favor. And therefore we have no satisfactory evidence to believe in their reality. Our safest course then is to admit the conclusion of eminent divines of different denominations, that miracles ceased with the first converts of the apostles.

Perhaps you believe in the divine inspiration of some one of the pretended prophets or christs. You know that many such have appeared in different ages of the church. Even now, we have a man in our own country, who declares that he is the very Christ; and pretends that he has come to judge the world. And strange as it may seem to us, he is attended by some respectable people who worship him as God. Some of these fanatics have obtained many converts; and there are various religious parties who still adhere to their teachings. If you are a believer in the divine mission of any one of this class, on what evidence is your faith founded? Certainly not on the gospel. For Jesus gives you no reason to expect any further revelation from heaven. Nay, he expressly forbids the indulgence of any such expectation. He plainly informs you that false Christs and false prophets would appear and deceive many. He solemnly cautions you not to be led astray by their devices and pretensions. And he has given you no authority to expect his second appearance until the grand consummation of all things; so that your belief must be unscriptural.—Do you found your belief on the bare word of a pretended messenger from heaven? This you cannot rationally do. For the word of one such person is as valuable as that of another. The honesty and sincerity of one are no more to be doubted than those of another. Several have appeared and made pretensions to a divine commission. Now the word of all cannot be received. For they all differ from each other in their instructions. They all promulgate a different system of faith and practice. So that you can found no belief on the bare word of a fanatic.—Do you rely on the state of feeling produced by a reception of the speculations of the pretended prophet? This you cannot rationally do. For every class of religionists confidently appeal to their feelings, in proof of the truth of their peculiar sentiments. This is done by the Jew, the Hindoo, the Mahometan, the Catholic, the Calvinist, the Methodist, the Universalist. And why are not the feelings of one man as good evidence in this case as those of another. They are. And if you admit this, you destroy this ground of belief. For all religions cannot be true. But such is human nature that persons of any sentiments can eventually bring their feelings to coincide with their belief.—Do you found your belief on the internal evidence of the writings of any pretended prophet? Let us look to this species of proof. Take for instance the books of Swedenborg, since they may be readily examined. So far as his instructions coincide with the gospel, all is well ; but this does not prove a new revelation. Where they extend beyond the teachings of scripture, some of them appear to me to be rational, some plausible, some ridiculous, some absurd, and some blasphemous. Where they contradict the precepts of the Bible, they appear to me to lead to the most dangerous results. He tells us that about one seventh part of the Old Testament, and more than one half of the New, are not the word of God. He allows us to keep concubines, and to put away our wives for trifling causes. He says many things on the connexion of the sexes which delicacy forbids me to mention, but which may be seen in his treatise on conjugial and scortatory love. Now this circumstance destroys all the proof arising from internal evidence. For surely God would not commission his son to reveal one system of practical truths, and another person to abolish them for the gratification of sensual lusts and appetites. So that the internal evidence of his writings is far from convincing me of their divine origin. And the same remarks are equally applicable to every system which has appeared since the completion of the New Testament. Let us then adhere to the rock of ages. Depart from Jesus, and follow any other guide, either nature, reason, pretended reformer, false prophet, or antichrist, and you but wander in midnight darkness.

III. What are some of the pernicious effects of popular superstitions?

1. They have caused a great waste of time. Look at the practices of heathen nations. Their religious ceremonies

are altogether superstitious. And consequently, all the time devoted to false gods must be considered as wasted. —Take a survey also of Catholic countries. During the dark ages, their priests were engaged in nonsensical disputes. Treatise after treatise was composed on such subjects as the following. How many angels can stand on the point of a needle? Have spirits any navels? Was Jesus Christ born totally depraved? Is the Virgin Mary the mother of God? And a thousand others equally senseless and unprofitable. In their monasteries, multitudes passed their days in repeating unintelligible prayers, poring over the legends of their saints, cutting figures in paper, and tormenting their bodies for the good of their souls.—Turn your attention likewise to Protestant lands. You learn that many a folio has been written on foolish and unintelligible subjects; that many a day has been occupied in trying and burning witches and heretics; that many a pharisaic custom has been scrupulously observed; and many an absurd opinion advanced and defended. And even in our own times, do you find no moments and hours occupied, in discoursing about signs and tricks, dreams and visions, spectres and apparitions?—In consulting charms, and lots, and fortune-tellers?—In prying into future events and occurrences?—In borrowing trouble on account of some supposed unfavorable omen?— Or in various other practices equally vain and superstitious? Now all this is wrong. Time is given for no such purposes. We have but a short period to remain in this world, and a great work to accomplish. Let us then be always engaged in something useful and virtuous.

2. Popular superstitions have also caused a great waste of human life. Cast your eye over the page of history.

You there notice an account of the trial by ordeal. This was effected both by fire and water. The accused person was required, either to hold red hot iron balls in his naked hands, or to walk over red hot plates of iron with bare feet. If he escaped unburned, he was considered innocent; but if he was scorched, sentence of death was pronounced. Or he was compelled, either to thrust his arm into a cauldron of boiling water; or be thrown into a deep pond. If he was either unscalded or drowned, his innocence was proved; but if he was scalded or could swim, the sentence of condemnation was passed. You perceive that in neither case, could life be saved, except by the interposition of a miracle; and this was not to be expected on such occasions. And through this superstition, thousands perished in this unrighteous manner.—You also notice the condemnations upon suspicion. Let the masonic knights be selected as an appropriate illustration. During the crusades, they constituted a large and important body. When the holy wars were over, they were accused, by some enemies, of every imaginable crime. The accusation was supported by no evidence whatever; for their lives were irreproachable. They were however condemned by their respective governments, without any proper trial, simply because they held secret meetings. Pardon was offered to all who would confess themselves guilty of the alleged crimes; while those, who would not make such a confession, were ordered to be burned to death in a slow fire of green wood. While all the villains escaped unharmed, large numbers of the virtuous were thus inhumanly murdered upon bare suspicion.— You notice likewise, the condemnations upon false evidence. The trials for witchcraft afford a good exemplification. I suppose the same evidence, upon which they were condemned to death, might now be brought against every old woman in the land. A distinguished writer computes that more than one hundred thousand persons of all ages have suffered death for witchcraft. Only think! one hundred thousand persons murdered by christian hands for a crime of which no human being was ever guilty!—You notice, finally, the condemnations for virtue. It is a duty to search the scriptures thoroughly, and abide by the results of the investigation. But for performing this sacred duty, professing Christians have murdered each other without mercy and without number. In our free republic, I trust that life cannot be destroyed without fair trial. But there are some few among us who pretend to believe, that all who do not think exactly as they do on certain subjects, must be eternally damned. So long however as they persecute only by words and curses, they are welcome to the happiness of such a belief. We are not to be judged by such weak minds, but by the unerring Jehovah. There are others who bring upon themselves sickness and even death, by their belief in signs, and dreams, and forewarnings. This glance at the historian's page should teach us never to expect a miracle in attestation of innocence; and never to condemn others, either on suspicion or on false evidence, or for doing the same things we practise ourselves.

8. Popular superstitions have caused much misery. We need not refer to history for an illustration of this assertion. We have sufficient examples around us. Look into society, and you will find one class, who pay particular attention to all signs and dreams. If anything unfavorable is indicated, their feelings are greatly depress-

ed; and if the contrary, they are as much elated. If a little insect, called the deathwatch, knocks for its mate on the wall, sleepless nights are sure to follow. If they notice the new moon over the wrong shoulder, their comfort is destroyed for a whole month. If they dream of death, they must send a letter forthwith to all absent relatives, even if they be settled in every state in the union.—You also notice another class, whose belief in the supernatural origin of omens and warnings leads them to adopt measures for their speedy fulfilment. Many a wedded couple seem to think they must quarrel, because they were married on a stormy day; and when some subject of dispute arises between them, they fall to fighting to prove the truth of the prediction. And for all this interruption of domestic harmony, they blame, not their own tempers and passions, but the decrees of fate. Many a person has supposed he must live in poverty, because a few moles have appeared on the wrong side of his body. And hence he neglects all industry and economy, and dissipates his time, and privileges, and talents.—You notice likewise a third class, who give themselves to tricks, fortune telling and opening books, to discover the events of futurity. Their spirits vary with the supposed indications of good or evil occurrences. A lady, who moved in the first circles, was once visiting in a clergyman's family of my acquaintance; and it was her regular morning practice, to toss up a little box of pins, and make her happiness for the day depend upon their accidental variation in falling. If they came down more heads than points, she was cheerful and happy; but if the contrary, she was gloomy and wretched. It seemed she valued her comfort, worth at least a brass pin. Many a worthy Christian has not only been deprived of his happiness, but betrayed into wild, extravagant, foolish, and sinful acts, by attempting to follow the suggestion of the passage which first meets his eye on opening his Bible. Many a poor wight has formed a disadvantageous matrimonial alliance, because some old hag has described black eyes and rosy cheeks as the characteristics of his future bride.—You notice, moreover a fourth class, who are for ever anticipating some dreadful calamity. Let any fool solemnly proclaim that war, famine or pestilence is approaching, they will give more heed to it than to that holy word which assures us that our heavenly Father will never leave nor forsake us. All uncommon appearances in the heavens, they look upon as indications of the threatened judgments of an angry God. Even the beautiful aurora borealis which spanned the blue concave above us was so interpreted. And even some clergymen, who should have known better, took occasion from it to terrify timid souls into an assent to their creeds.—Finally, you notice a fifth class, who exhibit the most wobegone countenances, and speak in the most sepulchral tones, and dole out their melancholy warnings to every cheerful spirit, and all for what? Why they fear that the universal Father will not eventually do so well for his children, as they would do for the human family, were their ability equal to their inclination. On account of this fear, they constantly torment themselves, and the smoke of their torments is continually ascending, to the great annoyance of all within the sphere of their influence.—Now all this is wicked. To permit any such superstition to disturb and destroy our enjoyment, is sin against heaven. Our heavenly Father created us for happiness. He has furnished us with the capacities and means of felicity. He has even commanded us to rejoice in the Lord always. He has given us a religion to effect this desirable object. It is as much a part of this religion to be always cheerful, contented and happy, as to be always temperate, just and virtuous. And if people would take one tenth part the pains to make themselves happy that they do to render themselves miserable, there would be ten times the present amount of happiness.

4. Popular superstitions have greatly injured the cause of medicine.—That superstition which leads people to believe in the efficacy of charms is very injurious. Let me explain my meaning by a few examples. The scrofula is frequently called the king's evil. It received this name because it was generally believed that the touch of a king would cure the disorder. This belief was formerly so prevalent, that the kings of England set apart one day in seven to bestow healing mercies on their subjects. The practice was begun in the year one thousand and fifty one, and continued until the reign of the present royal family, who were possessed of too much sense to encourage such an idle superstition. In the course of twentyseven years, there came to the first Charles to receive his touch, ninetytwo thousand one hundred and seven. In that country, the opinion still prevails, that the disorder can be cured by the touch of the ninth son of a ninth son ; and in our land, the seventh son of a seventh son.—Not long since, the cold hands of a convict, who had terminated his life on the gallows in Liverpool, were drawn over several wens a number of times, to effect a cure.—A person in one of our western states

lately run a pitchfork into his hand, and he applied a plaster to the cold iron as well as to the fresh wound. When people run a nail into their foot, they frequently save and polish the rusty iron to facilitate the recovery.—During the last season, in Maine, the body of a female was taken from the grave, her heart taken out and pulverised, and given to another member of the family as a specific for consumptive complaints. Did my limits permit, I could relate a thousand more cases equally silly and disgusting. All such things I class together under the general name of charms; and I pronounce them to be gross superstitions. For a belief in their efficacy implies one of three things. You may contend that there is healing efficacy in the prescriptions themselves. But this appears to me perfectly absurd. For you may as well have the touch of a slave as a king; you may as well apply your plaster to a tree as a pitchfork; you may as well drink the heart of a lamb as a woman.—You may say that God has determined certain cures shall follow certain applications. No such determination is published in his word. And no such conclusion can be inferred from facts.—You may pretend a special miracle is wrought on each occasion. But this is incredible. For the object is not worthy the miraculous interposition of the Deity. And the few cures which are reputed to have taken place, are satisfactorily accounted for on the influence of the imagination, and other natural causes. So that such a belief is not only superstitious, but calculated to lead people to neglect the proper means of recovery, and thus injure themselves and the medical profession.

That superstition which leads people to employ quack

doctors is also injurious to the cause of medicine. By a quack, I mean one who has not used the necessary means for obtaining a knowledge of the healing art. Many such have appeared in our country, and they may be divided into four classes. In the first place, there is the quack who depends for his success on the influence of imagination. Of this number was the famous Austin, who resided in Colchester, Vermont, about twenty years since. He proclaimed to the world that he could heal all *curable* diseases, if the suffering would give him a statement of their cases, either in person or by letter. He was visited by hundreds of invalids; and thousands more honored him with a written account of their afflictions. Reports of the most wonderful cures were put in circulation. But after a few years, the people discovered their folly, and permitted the pretended prophet to sink into his former merited obscurity.—In the second place, there is the quack who effects his cures by diet and regimen. Of this number was the celebrated rain water doctor. He established himself one time at Providence, and at another in this vicinity. Many of us can recollect the accounts of marvellous cures, and the flocking of invalids of all descriptions to his temple of health. He enjoined a spare diet, proper exercise, and suitable precaution; and in this way benefited many. But the community at length discovered the imposition; and left him to the undisturbed enjoyment of his rain water and his gruel.—In the third place, there is the quack who produces a temporary relief in chronic disorders, by the use of stimulating medicines. He actually raises the patient and makes him believe that his recovery is nearly effected. He then leaves him with orders to observe most sacredly certain directions. As soon as the stimulants have lost their power, a reaction takes place, and the patient sinks back to his former state. The quack immediately attributes this to some deviation from the prescriptions. And the patient is left either to linger on in wretchedness, or to give up the ghost, with the bitter reflection that his own negligence has hastened his dissolution.—Finally, there is the quack who either kills or cures with the most powerful remedies. Of this number is the notorious Thompson of lobelia memory. You often observe notices of deaths which are declared to be caused by the prescriptions of some of his disciples. For my own part, I have no doubt these are generally true. I do not suppose they kill their patients intentionally, but in pure ignorance.—Now I must consider it superstition which leads to the employment of such characters. Do you suppose God assists them by miracle? This is absurd. Do you suppose he has miraculously given them that knowledge which others acquire only by long and close study and practice? This is equally absurd. Do you suppose they prescribe by guess, and cure by accident? This is doubtless the truth. How absurd, then, to give them employment. Should you call me foolish were I to employ a Hottentot to instruct my children?—An American savage to defend my civil rights?—And a Hindoo to preach for my edification? And how much more superstitious should I prove myself were I to employ a person to tamper with my very life, who I knew had never taken the proper measures for acquiring a knowledge of the human system, its various diseases and their appropriate remedies.

That superstition which would prevent human dissections, is likewise injurious to the cause of medicine. In France provision is made by law for securing a proper supply of subjects. Those who die in prisons, hospitals, and alms-houses are consigned to the medical faculty, unless claimed within a certain time by some friend. In Great Britain, no such law exists; and the difficulty of obtaining subjects has been so great, as not only to injure the science, but to induce the physicians of Scotland to agree to give up their own bodies for dissection. An attempt is now making in Parliament to obtain the passage of some law by which the present evil may be obviated. In our country, no law exists on this subject; and there prevails a very general opposition to obtaining subjects in any manner. This arises from two causes. In the first place, many people believe in the literal resurrection of this animal body; and therefore they are unwilling to have it exposed to the dissecting knife. Now supposing this belief is true, what harm can follow from the dissection. Will not the Almighty be able to collect and unite its scattered dust and fragments? To suppose the contrary, would be impeaching his omniscience and omnipotence. But for my own part, I believe with St Paul, that flesh and blood cannot inherit the kingdom of God. My present body is composed of flesh, and blood, and bones. Of course, it can be of no use to me after death. While I remain in this world, I will make it as serviceable as possible. When I leave it, if it can be of any value to my fellow beings, I cheerfully consign it to their service. After they have taken to pieces the curious workmanship of the Almighty, and obtained such knowledge as may enable them to be useful in their profession, I hope they will give the fragments a decent burial, and refrain from disturbing the feelings of any surviving friend. When I enter upon the next stage of existence, I firmly trust my heavenly Father will give me a spiritual body, adapted to the wants and improvements of my immortal soul. And if people will examine the scriptures more carefully on this point, and realize the importance of having a proper supply of subjects, I have no doubt they will generally coincide with my views and declarations.—The second cause of opposition is such as we can all appreciate. None of us wish to know that the remains of our departed friends have been disturbed. This is a sacred sentiment, and it should be respected. And for this reason, that we may be delivered from fear on this subject, our government is called upon to make some legal provision for the necessary supply. This is the only thing that can save our feelings, and promote the science of medicine. I suppose every person of common sense knows that subjects must be dissected. Would you employ a person to put a watch together who had never seen one taken apart? And can you expect a person to understand surgery and medicine without an intimate acquaintance with the human body?

5. Popular superstitions have greatly injured the cause of pure religion.—That superstition which allows any substitute for personal righteousness is very pernicious. The Pharisees considered themselves holy, because they were descendants of faithful Abraham. They also fasted twice a week; paid tithes of all they possessed; made long prayers in public places; were zealous to gain proselytes to their party, and strictly observed all sacred days and ceremonial observances. At the same

time, they neglected the weightier matters of the law, justice, mercy and faithfulness; devoured widows' houses, and were proud, bigoted and self-righteous.—Some Roman Catholics perform tedious pilgrimages; lacerate their bodies most inhumanly; abstain from meats and drinks on certain days; pay the priests and the pope for the pardon of their sins, and bequeath their property to the church. At the same time, they indulge in false-hoods, profanity, intemperance, debauchery, and other heinous iniquities.—Some Protestants attend punctually upon all religious meetings; subscribe to contradictory articles of belief; compass sea and land to make con-verts to their denomination; observe all gospel ordi-nances, and exhibit great sanctity of outward appearance. At the same time, they are fretful, unkind and disobliging in their families; censorious in their conversation; un-charitable in their judgment; grasping in their dealings, and unhappy in their dispositions. Others pretend to be-lieve, either that they are of the number of the elect, and therefore cannot commit iniquity; or that Christ has died for the sins of the whole world, and therefore they may continue sinning with impunity; or that if they ex-hibit an outward form of godliness, their hearts may be filled with avarice, ambition, lust, revenge, and impiety. All such substitutes for personal goodness, I class to-gether. And I pronounce them to be superstitions, be-cause they derive no support from reason, experience or revelation. A belief in them is exceedingly injurious to the cause of piety and holiness; because it leads people to neglect the one thing needful, a uniformly sober, right-eous and godly life. God will assuredly render unto every man according to his deeds. Be he pharisee or sadducee, catholic or protestant, orthodox or liberal, elect or nonelect, he can escape the punishment of no sin, except by reformation. And no sin is ever removed, no virtue is ever given, by miracle. Our iniquities must be forsaken, and our goodness acquired, by our own exertions, aided by the promised influence of the holy spirit. And until we have accomplished both these objects, we cannot rationally expect any pure and permanent happiness.

That superstition which leads people to believe in the miraculous powers of the devil is also very pernicious in its consequences. This belief was retained by some of the early reformers, among other heathen and popish absurdities. Martin Luther gravely informs us that his satanic majesty entered his bolted chamber one night, stole his hazelnuts, and cracked them on his bed-post, to his no small annoyance; and that he appeared to him on another occasion, in the form of Jesus Christ, suspended on the cross. And he would have us believe that the old dragon was leagued with the catholic church, and tormented him because he was engaged in reforming her abuses. But many persons of the present day are so skeptical, as to think his devils were occasioned by nothing worse than good living and the want of proper exercise.—In the time of New England witchcraft, Cotton Mather took home one of the possessed damsels, to learn the ways and works of satan. He discovered, that while her devil would neither permit her to hear his prayers nor read the scriptures, he was much pleased to have her peruse any quaker publication, and especially the episcopalian prayer book; thus modestly intimating that while quakerism and episcopalianism were under the special patronage of the evil one, he was exceedingly opposed to calvinism; and if he is a personage of such understanding as his friends represent, I am not surprised that he was a little shocked at some of the representations this system gives of the character and proceedings of the universal Creator.—Not long since, a house in Maine was said to be haunted. The building and furniture were shaken, dreadful noises were heard, dismal sights were seen, and heavy blows were received. The occupant of the house had lately left a calvinistic theological seminary. He is now a settled universalist preacher. Since his change of sentiments, he has explained to the people the probable causes of the disturbances. A neighboring family informed me, that he now considered it the spirit of God, haunting him to forsake calvinism and declare universal salvation. His explanation is just as satisfactory as those of Luther and Mather. Whoever understands the influence of the imagination, will find no difficulty in accounting for the occurrences in either case.—An anonymous writer has lately given us some information on the miraculous powers of the devil. By adopting a literal interpretation of some figurative passages of scripture, he pretends to believe the old serpent stood on a high mountain, and actually surveyed all the kingdoms of this round world. What wonderful powers of vision, to see either through this solid globe eight thousand miles; or around it twentyfive thousand! But this is not all. He teaches that Christ Jesus is the very God, and that his agony in the garden was caused by a fight with old beelzebub. Who can tell but this powerful prince of darkness will some day or other obtain the victory, and take the government of the universe into his own hands! But to crown the whole, in the true spirit of the dark ages, he would have us know that all who do not receive his interpretations of scripture, as infallible, are the very advocates and emissaries of satan. Now I frankly confess that my Maker has not given me a believing faculty sufficiently capacious to receive such enormous truths. And if a literal meaning is to be given to all the figurative parts of scripture, I must give up the expectation of becoming orthodox in my sentiments.— I once resided in a place where there was a very general awakening. In a few months I discovered that the largest portion of the converts, and especially the most zealous, had fallen from grace, to be great workers of iniquity. I inquired the cause of so singular an occurrence, and was informed by a deacon, that all such were the devil's converts, and that he usually secured a larger number in revivals of religion than the Lord.—Not many years ago, a man was suddenly missing from a certain town in this commonwealth. The church immediately sent one of her members to consult the far famed fortune telling Molly Pitcher. After making the necessary inquiries, she intimated that the absent person had been murdered by a family of negroes, and his body sunk in the deep waters behind their dwelling. Upon this evidence, the accused were forthwith imprisoned, and the pond raked in vain from shore to shore. A few days previous to the trial, the murdered man returned to his friends safe and sound; thus giving the naughty skeptics occasion to say, that the fortune teller, instead of receiving from the devil information of distant and future events, had actually played the very devil with the superstitious church.—These examples are enough to show you that a belief in the miraculous powers of the devil is still prevalent in the land. And it is very injurious to the cause of pure religion, because it leads people to be watching for the assaults of an outward tempter when they should be disciplining their inward lusts and passions; because it furnishes the sinner with a very convenient packhorse for his iniquities; because it fills the timid soul with fears of imaginary dangers; because it keeps alive an eager credulity for every tale of ignorance and superstition; because it gives religious partizans the opportunity of accusing their opponents of being under satanic influence, and because it turns the thoughts from an all perfect being who regulates the minutest events, to a malignant leader of a hellish host. And when such impressions are made upon the minds of children, the effect is most baneful and lasting. A pious mother not finding it convenient to attend her little son to rest, told him to omit his prayers for one night. "Mother," said the child, "will the devil forgive me if I neglect my prayers?" Resist the devil and he will flee from thee.

That superstition which leads people to believe that God works miracles at the present day, is likewise very injurious to the cause of religion. This belief is also a remnant of popery. In the Roman church, miracles are of common occurrence. The priests are able to get them up on almost any emergency. Prince Hohenloe has lately cured another case of the consumption by his prayers. Many impositions have doubtless been practiced on the ignorant and credulous Catholics; but we must resort to the influence of the imagination for a satisfactory explanation of some of their pretended miracles.—The preachers in some christian denominations, pretend to inspiration. Their hearers really believe that the thoughts of their discourses are immediately suggested to their minds by the holy spirit. If so, then they indeed proclaim a new revelation. But to me it seems impious to attribute such confused, fanatical harangues to the fountain of wisdom, and truth, and purity. I am sure I should never mistake them for the dictates of divine inspiration. If you listen to the experiences which are related by applicants for church membership, you will find that many of them are nothing less than miraculous. My limits will permit me to record but one case, which occurred in a late revival. The man went to bed an unconverted sinner. His body soon began to swell, and continued increasing, until it reached the size of a hogshead. A bright light then filled the chamber, and Christ Jesus appeared. The swelling began to subside immediately, and all settled down in his heart. He arose in the morning, a regenerated Christian. I am sorry that ministers, who know how to account for these vain imaginations, permit their converts to relate them as evidences of their regeneration.—Some persons believe that a *chemical* change is produced on their hearts by the miraculous influence of the spirit. Their belief is acquired by receiving literally, the figurative expressions of their preachers. I have conversed with several such characters. We cannot be too plain and perspicuous in our discourses. The expressions frequently used in seasons of religious excitement, are liable to the same objection. We hear that the Almighty is visiting such a town; that he is coming this way; that he has arrived in a certain village; that he will remain but a few days longer; that he has been driven away by unbelievers, and that he cannot be expected again for many years. Such language is not only false, but shocking to my mind, in the highest degree. Our heavenly Father is everywhere present. He never leaves nor forsakes his children. He is more ready to give his holy spirit, than earthly parents to give good gifts to their offspring. He is always ready to assist those who assist themselves; but not in a miraculous manner.—Now a belief in modern miracles is unsupported by evidence. And it injures the cause of truth and righteousness; because it leads ignorant persons to mistake the suggestions of their own hearts for the miraculous operations of the holy spirit; because it encourages sinners to defer attention to the duties of religion, in expectation of the special interposition of heaven; because it induces new converts to disregard the only scriptural evidence of conversion, a sober, righteous and godly life, and enables them to feel satisfied with certain impulses, resolutions, and opinions; because it gives encouragement to every illiterate fanatic or designing hypocrite to demand the belief of a credulous community, and because it weakens and destroys the foundation of belief in those miracles which were wrought for the establishment of revelation.

We talk much about the march of mind; and it certainly has moved several steps. We boast greatly of our enlightened land; and in comparison with other nations, we are enlightened. We are abundantly favored with advantages for mental and moral instruction. We are signally blessed with literary and religious privileges. But with all our opportunities for information, I fear we have some ignorance and superstition remaining. I suspect it would be no difficult task to bring back the days of persecution and witchcraft in some circles. Let them be made to believe, that the devil works miracles, that witches exist, and that all who differ from them in opinion on religious subjects are under satanic influence. Let them be made to believe, that all the religious excitements and commotions of the present day are occasioned by the miraculous effusions of the holy spirit; and that all excited feelings, dreams, visions, and the like, are sure indications of the electing grace of the Almighty. Let them be made to believe, that it is their duty to hate all whom God hates, and that He hates all who will not embrace their creeds. Let them believe, that they must punish all who depart from the faith of the pilgrims. Let these sentiments be reduced to practice, and trials for heresy, blasphemy, and witchcraft would once more disgrace the annals of our nation. But, thanks to God, a better day has dawned. A spirit of inquiry is abroad. Power is in the hands of liberal spirits. And the remaining superstitions of popery are fast following the numberless exploded absurdities of the dark ages, into the ocean of oblivion. Let us lend a helping hand to hasten the downfall of ignorance, error, and sin; and promote the universal reign of knowledge, truth, and holiness. .

IV. What means can we adopt for the banishment of popular superstitions?

1. We must first deliver ourselves from their domination; for we are all more or less under their influence. When any of the common signs of good or evil fortune appear before us, our thoughts involuntarily recur to the things supposed to be signified. Sometimes a momentary shudder is communicated to the whole system; occasion-

ally a feeling of unnatural exultation is awakened; unpleasant sensations are often excited; and frequently, a depression of spirits is produced. And how can we escape from such thraldom? By the exercise of our reason. We are indeed taught by the ancient proverb, that we must not expect to reason out what was never reasoned in. Yet such old sayings do not always prove correct in this age of discoveries and improvements. And I am confident that a proper use of our reasoning faculties will enable us to accomplish this undertaking. We must convince ourselves that all these things are the offspring of ignorance; that they have no foundation in reason, philosophy, or religion; and that they are exceedingly pernicious in their consequences. When fully persuaded of these truths, we must strive to make our feelings coincide with the dictates of our understandings. And this we can effect by persevering self-discipline. Such exertions will eventually deliver us from the inconvenience, vexation, and slavery of popular superstitions.

2. We must also assist our fellow men in the performance of this great and good work. We often meet with those who are firm believers in signs and dreams, in fortune-telling and witchcraft, in apparitions and ghosts. We must endeavor to convince them that no dependence whatever can be placed on any of these vanities; that they are all fictions, absurdities, and evils. And if we cannot produce conviction by sober sense and sound argument, I think we shall be justified in this particular case, in resorting to ridicule. In one or the other of these ways, we may hope to give a new turn to discourse. For much time is now spent, in many a family circle, in enumerating the various signs, in explaining the different

tricks, in relating dreams, and in detailing stories of haunted houses, hobgoblins, and devils. In this way, the evil is cherished, and transmitted from generation to generation. But if we can give an opposite direction to conversation; if we can induce people to reason about these things, and inquire into their origin, causes, and effects, and investigate the evidence on which they are supposed to rest, and adopt rational conclusions, we shall be usefully employed. For this course will eventually lead to the banishment of popular superstitions.

3. We must likewise attend to the early education of our children. For it is during infancy and childhood that our heads are filled with marvellous stories. They are told to us by some of those persons to whose care we are early entrusted, either to frighten us into obedience, or to gratify our thirst for the new and the wonderful, or to while away a tedious evening, or to relieve their own overflowing imaginations. They sink deep into our confiding hearts, and leave impressions the most pernicious and the most lasting. Could a child be educated without any knowledge of such things, he would never be troubled with their baneful influence. Our duty is therefore plain. If we take the principal care of our children ourselves, we should not permit them to learn anything of such vanities from our lips; and our daily conduct should evince that they exert no influence on our feelings, or conduct, or happiness. If any of us employ other persons to be with our offspring in early life, we must charge them to conceal everything of the kind from their knowledge; and we should regard a disobedience of this command as a most heinous offence. After our children are of sufficient age to associate with others, we

must caution them to avoid believing or relating any superstitious tales, as they would shun known falsehoods. If we persevere in this practice, we shall save them from the degrading influence of popular superstitions.

4. We must moreover endeavor to increase the means of public education. For you generally find that the most enlightened are the most free from superstition, and consequently, a high degree of mental cultivation would effect a general deliverance. And how can we accomplish this grand object? Are any satisfied with our present literary advantages? Let us reason with them on the value and importance of knowledge. Let us show them, by an appeal to facts, that all our civil, social, domestic and religious blessings, depend for their very existence on the intelligence and virtue of the people. Do any complain of the scarcity of money and the want of funds? Let us show them, by an appeal to facts, that more money is annually wasted in all our towns, either in extravagant living, dress, furniture and equipage; or in shows, amusements, balls and pleasure parties; or in gaming, dissipation, lottery tickets, military parades, and spiritous liquors,—than is expended for the instruction of the rising generation. No. There is no want of funds. When there is a will, there is a way. The importance of this subject is not generally understood. Almost everything else seems of more consequence than learning and wisdom. This will never answer. The world is growing wiser. Those who will not employ the requisite means, must rest contented with comparative ignorance. Let us not be of this unworthy number. If we feel the importance of a change in these respects, let us persevere in our laudable exertions. Let us leave no objections

unanswered, no arguments unused, no measures untried, until we succeed in obtaining the means of giving all our children a high degree of education. And whoever shall live to see such a result, will behold the almost universal banishment of popular superstition.

5. Finally, we must labor for the diffusion of pure and undefiled religion. Let us adhere to the plain teachings of Jesus. And then we shall believe that there is but one self-existent, undivided, all perfect, all pervading spirit; and that He is truly the merciful, loving, unchangeable parent of all his human children. We shall believe, that he alone regulates all the events of this world which are above our control; and that all his various dispensations originate in wisdom and benevolence. We shall believe that Jesus of Nazareth is really the anointed Son of God; and the commissioned and all-sufficient Saviour of the world. We shall believe that God made us for ever increasing and never ending happiness; and that we can secure this unspeakable favor, only by living soberly, righteously, and godly. We shall believe that we have no worse enemies than our own sins; and that power is given us to conquer these, even in the present existence. We shall believe that it is as much our duty to be always happy, as to be always honest; and that our heavenly Father has commissioned no fate, nor chance, nor witches, nor devils, to torment us. If we live up to this belief, we shall secure a large share of temporal enjoyment, and be prepared for the increasing felicity of the spiritual world. And if we produce this state of faith and ractice] in ourselves and all around us, we shall have done much for the banishment of popular superstitions.